seeing the signs

spirituality of the ordinary

PAUL KOCAK

Kocak Wordsmiths Ink

Kocak Wordsmiths Ink
347 Whittier Avenue
Syracuse, NY 13204

Cover Art and Interior Layout
Becky Bayne, Becky's Graphic Design
www.beckysgraphicdesign.com

For John Giuliani, Joe Bergin,
and Georgina Hegney

PAUL KOCAK

INTRODUCTION

THE SIGNS ARE EVERYWHERE. What are we to make of the signs around us? It's a simple question with not-so-simple answers. On one level, we can dodge the question every moment of every day. Life is life. Reality is reality. There are no "signs" to interpret, no "meaning" to divine. Everything is just as it is, requiring no intervention of thought or assigned significance. On another plane, signs are everywhere. Just as soothsayers or prophets of old discovered meaning in entrails or saw signs in dreams, so might we. The Emperor Constantine blazed his

SEEING THE SIGNS

"in hoc signo vinces," or "in this sign you will conquer," Christian vision into the annals of Western history. From a modern perspective, are Sigmund Freud or Carl Jung any more or less an authority on interpreting our waking, or sleeping, lives?

This is risky business. See a meaning-laden "sign" in every quotidian gesture and you might find yourself in the realm of psychosis or paranoia. Is this what mystics, saints, and seers faced? Is one person's dabbling in astrological signs another person's surrender of will and purpose?

These miniatures are one person's observations of daily life. I compiled them from my blog, The Laughorist, mostly unedited and mostly in reverse chronological order, most recent first. Don't take them too seriously. God knows, I haven't. Rather, see them as invitations to give you pause. May they spur you to stop, look, and listen to the world before us. If you find some of the delight that has surprised me, I trust we will both be grateful.

Paul Kocak

Syracuse, New York

February 23, 2015

PAUL KOCAK

CONTENTS

SEEING THE SIGNS

FICTION
BEGINS HERE

MY OL' BALTIMORE CATECHISM declared that a sacrament is "an outward sign of God's love." Something along those lines. Speaking of signs, of God's love or otherwise, I saw this sign at the Central Library branch of the Onondaga County Public Libraries, in downtown Syracuse, on the fourth floor:

FICTION BEGINS HERE

Hmmmmm. Well, at least the sign wasn't on the non-fiction floor. How mystifying. "Fiction begins here." We can all use overt warnings now and then. I mean, we don't always get such explicit declarations. For example, many folks entering a marriage or other such relationship would welcome such a disclaimer. At least you'd know what you were in for. "Fiction Begins Here." That would also work on the boss's door. Or even on the top of the annual so-called performance evaluation form, in bold italic underscore all uppercase. "Fiction Begins Here" should be the standard crawl on the bottom of the television screen when certain public officials are speaking (for my money, notably reserved for jowly, white-shirted, obstructionists protecting their greed). "Fiction Begins Here." It's a handy sign, sacramental or otherwise.

SEEING THE SIGNS

PRESENCE

I SAW A SIGN IN FRONT OF ST. ANN CHURCH, just outside the City of Syracuse -- "in the world but not of it," you might say, if you are not suburban-minded (as I am not).

The sign read:

LESS PRESENTS
MORE PRESENCE

I liked it. I like it.

Did the pastor give a Christmas homily on that?

It's a facile declaration. Simple.

But what would it mean? Fewer physical gifts and more staring into eyes, more hugs and holding hands?

I talk a good game.

This would be harder than I thought.

THE HEALING TOUCH

YOU GOT THERE LATE, as is your habit, character flaw, or constant misjudgment of time constraints. St. Paul's Cathedral. Downtown Syracuse. The Hadley Chapel, a dusty taste of Olde England or late 1800s America. Four men, including yourself, scattered in straightback, wicker chairs, a priest at the altar. She invites all to join her around the table. Communion. Co-union. Eucharist. Thanks. The men look sad, you think, but upon reflection find that a misperception. Sadness, yes, but a calm; subtle smiles, serenity, a hunger. A sense of spiritual surrender perfumes the air like incense. After the Eucharist, the priest asks you, "Do you want the healing? You were late, and . . ." "Sure, I'm always up for some healing," you interrupt (another habit or flaw or branding characteristic). She walks up to the front. You kneel at the communion railing with its cushions. The priest, who happens to be the rector of the Cathedral parish, tells you how even if you were not present earlier, the fruits of the healing service are yours to taste. She has a small container in her hands, the holy chrism. She asks if there is any need or person you want to mention, on whose behalf you want healing extended. You are caught by surprise. You can't speak.

You can name (or not name) dozens of
people, endless needs, candidates for
unction, salve, and balm. The emotion
embarrasses you and you check it, contain
it, at least outwardly. "Josephine," you say.
"My mom, 98," you get out. The priest
anoints your forehead with oil. Her hands
touch your forehead. She lays her hands
on your head, firmly. She holds her hands
on your hair, on your head, saying prayers
of healing, invoking Christ to heal, repair,
comfort. It's not so much the words. You
may even mishear the words. It is the
human touch that reaches you. You want
to empty yourself by sobbing, but you do
not. (How indecorous would it be?) But
this hearty touch. And when her hands lift,
you are lighter. Residual moisture rims the
corners of your eyes. Did she know? You
wondered, what if this were the moment

your mother died? Does it matter? All
would be well. All things would be well.

PAUL KOCAK

WHAT I SAW
TODAY

- **A FEW DOZEN VEHICLES EITHER OFF
  THE ROAD**, facing the wrong way,
  or on the road, same calamitous
  circumstances, owing to the slippery
  slope of snow

- whitened and crystalline branches,
  limbs, tree trunks, and mini-palisades

SEEING THE SIGNS

- rain or snow or ice against the windshield

- windshield wipers

- the tired yet wise and kind eyes of the 98-year-old woman who gave birth to me

- my hometown, remarkably recognizable

- toll booths

- lines of people at the rest stop, also called text stop

- road signs

- heavily mascaraed and tired-beyond-years eyes of a gas station sales clerk

- a McDonald's crispy chicken sandwich

- a holiday bouquet of not-very-fresh flowers

SEEING THE SIGNS

- a coffee-to-go, from Wendy's

- apostrophes

- the digital readout of mileage on my
  car's dashboard surpassing 100000

VULNERABLE ADULT

UPON ENTERING THE HIGHWAY, Route 690 West, I saw an electronic sign alerting motorists to a VULNERABLE ADULT. The sign identified a type of vehicle, possibly accompanied by a plate number. No disrespect or insensitivity intended toward the missing or unprotected "vulnerable adult," but the sign gave me pause. *Vulnerable Adult. vulnerable adult.* (With or without the initial caps, with or without the proprietary nomenclature.) Are you a vulnerable adult? Am I? Yes, we are all sometimes vulnerable adults. Some of us, all the time. And we are vulnerable to the slings of time, the arrows of circumstance or history. We are at risk to fame and fortune, or at peril to poverty and perdition. And when we find ourselves vulnerable as adults, either individually or collectively, who is there to shield or save us? Should they? How? Or should our vulnerability merely introduce us to the icons of impermanence, the faceless faces of Nirvana?

I kept driving.

MONARCHY; THE ROYAL OUI

I AM WALKING THE DOG. Is it my dog? She was. Or is. (Can anyone lay claim to *owning* a pet? How could this lovely, loyal friend be deemed a *possession?*) We are walking in Burnet Park, Syracuse, where we have walked dozens, probably hundreds, of times. It is daytime. We walk this route less frequently in the Time of Estrangement. October sunlight. An ample, warm breeze. We are walking on a modest incline toward the golf course clubhouse, toward O'Leary Drive, where in December the jangling bells and clipclop hooves of steaming horses will carry Christmas-celebrating families. Walking into the wind, I am arrested. (Not the dog; she keeps going, only halted by squirrels, who are busy and in abundance.) I am halted by the sight of one monarch butterfly riding the wind. I see it glide and loop for several seconds. Then it vanishes. Not seen. A vision in broad daylight. Monarch. From the Greek, one who rules alone. Ruling my field of vision, ruling my heart and its beats. A sacramental sign. A sign of what, you ask? Of is-ness. That. *Suchness*. Yes.

SEEING THE SIGNS

DEER ME

DRIVING HOME THE OTHER DAY, late afternoon, early evening (who can remember any more? maybe I am making all this up as I type), near the Syracuse border with Solvay, I saw a white-tailed deer gallop off to my right, into some shrubbery, fenced off. Did I say gallop? Gallop with a dollop of prance and hurdle and gambol and leap. Seconds later: a middle-aged bearded man riding a bicycle. I try to catch the eye of the bicyclist, as if to wordlessly say, "Dude, you see that? You see that deer? You chasing it?" Even if I did catch the bicyclist's eye for a split second, he wasn't indulging me. His look was like, "I'm riding this bike. Deer? I ain't seen no deer." I made the right turn. I thought I'd intersect the path of the deer, but no sign of it. In the bush, I guess. Or else it was a very large dog or a fox. Or a figment. (It's redundant redundant to say "figment of imagination.") A 3-D figment of fantasy. But naw. It was real. It was a deer. And don't tell me the bicyclist didn't see it. I'll wager the two of 'em, Bicycle Man and Deer Me, have this bit, this act they've worked out. It's a routine. "Figment Follies."

WHAT MELTS

IS IT MERELY THE TEMPERATURE OR A METAPHYSICAL THAW, all this melting, this evaporation, this trans-formation. Where does it all go? And what is 'it' we are referring to? Not that it is something 'less,' because nothing is lost, all is impermanent, the zen masters remind us. All is here, and nothing is lost; no-thing. In the vespers dusk, the scuds of clouds before this cafe window breeze leftward, it may be east or south, or both. These clouds (cumulus, stratus? cumulostratus? I forget my cloud taxonomy, from fourth grade; I need a nap, where different clouds can float by in front of a different sort of lens) of dusky gray lavender, ashy dustiness are already reshaped, gone, departed from what my fingers were tapping about moments ago. I do not lament them as lost, or found. Someone a few miles down the road is welcome to greet them.

The skeletal, bronchiated limbs of the winter trees across West Genesee Street stand silently before me. They too are as transient as those clouds above their sight line. Those slender naked branches are eloquent. I bow before them, and them before me.

SEEING THE SIGNS

LIVE NUDE FISH

I SAW THE SIGN ON ROUTE 298. LIVE NUDE FISH. On one of those little A-frame sign holders. It caught my eye. I don't deny it. And let's be honest, the FISH part was not the hook, shall we say. Echoes of the 1980s, working in Midtown Manhattan, before Times Square and its environs went all Disney on us. The neon signs then said LIVE NUDE GIRLS. Or am I misremembering the lures and bait that pedestrians faced? One had to be curious about the diction, the word choices, though. Several blocks from the literal Madison Avenue, the promoters of carnal license seemed to need no lessons in the ad game. The NUDE was an obvious allurement, as old as the hills (well, not the wording but the stark naked commercialism trading on human weakness; nothing new there), but LIVE? Surely, DEAD would be a turn-off, except for creepy necro types. Why not WOMEN? Too much Mrs. Robinson? Or MEN? Or ADULT PERSONS? With LIVE NUDE FISH we've come a long way, baby. Or have we? On a scale of 1 to 10, how far? Fin de siècle. Finis. Something's fishy here.

FOCUS

IT HAS BEEN said the whole universe is found in a drop of water. I saw it today. Extending my arm out the car window to send out some cards (hand-written communication? how quaint!), under the lower-right lip of the mailbox's mouth, one plump drop of rain held itself suspended (or was held suspended), waiting, frozen but melted, pausing, still.

SEEING THE SIGNS

WHAT I GOT (AND DIDN'T GET) FROM CHURCH

WE WERE LATE, after the Nicene Creed. But we were just as welcome whether we professed a set of any beliefs or not. Who is "we"? My daughter, 13; her friend, 14; and I, 61. Why were we late? (What is this, the Inquisition? The Inquisition is a favorite topic of anti-religionists, and rightly so. Of course, the anonymous touch of hospice caregivers, whether atheists or believers; the drunkards' welcome; the Samaritans' feeding of the hungry: these headline-hidden, quotidian acts are beyond inquisition and definition and category, but they are perhaps not as galvanizing for debate.) We were late owing to fatigue or lack of longing or just-plain habit or genetic determination. Go figure.

I wondered: Why here? Why now?

We had missed the Gospel. We did not hear the clarion call of good news, but our ears may have been too sleep-sodden to be roused. We heard no sermon. No one preached at us or to us. And I felt that as an absence, a missing out on erudition and insight.

As my mind wandered, looking out the window opening to the garden holding ashes of the dead and gone, the flowering crab apple, the trickling water, the redbud, in autumnal array — a place where I will "rest"? — I seized on the collective nature of the Eucharistic enterprise, the union of encomium. Where else do I (or anyone) do anything as a community? A sporting event, a lecture, a rally, a speech. Eating at the mall food court does not measure up to that. So, yes, we were there as a body, albeit with wandering minds and beliefs and disbeliefs and varying degrees of the discrete charms of the bourgeoisie. The same can be said of lemmings, you say? I'd have to research that. And can you tell me whether lemmings are "happy"?

The Eucharist itself was a salty bread, not the papery wafer of my youth, when it would stick to the roof of my mouth as stubbornly as papal bulls cling to dogma and doctrine. A shared and silent meal. A respite among the hungry, the tired, the poor in spirit. I sat in the pew after chewing and digesting this. And I tried to think of what? Nothing. Just tried to be grateful, in obedience to Eucharist's etymology, if nothing else.

And while we stood for the final hymn, I was suddenly nudged, elbowed by my daughter.

Look, and you shall see!

To the left, the shock of the new, or at least the unexpected: at first I figured it for a calico cat soft-pawing among

the dead, among the quick, among the
leaves of those left. But no! A red fox!
Vulpes vulpes. And then just as quickly
gone. An apparition? A natural nativity of
nowness? A benediction of *mirabile visu?*

Amen to this sacrament of the ordinary,
this all-too-predictable surprise brought to
us by St. Charles Darwin & Company Ltd.

SEEING THE SIGNS

SIGNAGE
MEDITATION

YOU SEE THE GATEWAY SIGN TO TIPPERARY HILL, at the near crest of a hill in front of All Saints Elementary School and Saint John the Baptist Ukrainian Catholic Church. The sign is a few yards in front of that Taras guy (whose last name escapes you and thank God his name is not in Cyrillic), the Ukrainian poet. Yes, Tipp Hill: not just for Irish-Americans. Ukrainian-Americans too. The letters forming "Welcome to Tipperary

Hill" (were those the words?) are faded from the sign. In fact, only your memory or your expectations fill in the gestalt emptiness of the sign, which has only faded traces of letters. Fill in the blanks, the sign seems to command you. And is such a ghostly sign a challenge or statement or reflection or editorial? And what is the content of that less-than-minimalist message? If the medium is the message, what is the medium? What sign is this? Saying what? If signs are sacraments, or sacraments signs, what does this implore us to conclude?

SEE: SEESAW SEEN

IN EAST SYRACUSE (why is there no South Syracuse or West Syracuse?) today, I saw a yellow-background traffic warning sign depicting a black seesaw, with a symbolic creature, presumably a child, on each side of the 45-degree angled plank. Seesaw, a simple reduplicative word, which can work as a verb, a noun, or an adjective.

I wonder. Why a seesaw warning sign?

Beware of hurling kids?

Prepare for economic turbulence?

After all, I was en route to the bank.

LESS THAN NOTHING

PICTURE THIS: A concrete abutment adjoining a railroad overpass, the concrete polished and new, in contrast to the rugged, rusted iron of the CSX railroad bridge over West Fayette Street, Syracuse, New York. Spray-painted in black upon this otherwise pristine urban whiteboard is a graffito of one word, perhaps one foot high, a yard wide:

N   O   T   H   I   N   G

What catches my eye is the gestalt of nothing, for the graffito is a piece of urban design that adds by subtraction. Each of those seven letters is less than a letter; each letter is truncated, almost overcome by silence and absence (and who isn't overcome now and then by silence or absence?). At first glance I don't see a word but a modern urban hieroglyphic.

Oh, you say, show us a photo. Show and tell!

Too easy.

Picture an N that almost looks like an upside-down V; an O reminiscent of a U; an H -- oh, stop! I can't tell you. I don't precisely remember. I cannot recount with confidence. Come on out and see this sub-nihilist shrine for yourself.

So, who is the author, the designer of Less Than Nothing? And what is he or she or they trying to tell us?

Is Less Than Nothing more sublime, more alluring than nothingness itself?

(Nothing has its semantic merits, as in signifying no-thing. The English language is great like that, as also demonstrated by the word atonement, at-one-ment.)

The signs are here for us to see, awaiting our meaning.

SIGN RIPOSTE

THIS SIGN SEEN ON one of those hand-drying devices featuring a revolving cloth towel:

WARNING: Use only to dry hands and face.

Any other use can be DANGEROUS.

1. Why "hands and face" and not "hands or face"?

2. Really?

3. Exactly what other use?

4. Did an attorney demand the installation of this sign?

5. What would Kierkegaard say?

6. What would Kierkegaard do?

SEEING THE SIGNS

UNCOMMON SCENTS

HANDWRITTEN SIGN SEEN today in bathroom of downtown Syracuse bagel shop:

Do not take air freshener

It has G.P.S.

We will track you down!

This raises the following intriguing questions:

1. Why no fuss over the theft of the missing period in line 1?

2. If there has been a rash of bathroom air fresheners stolen from this location, what is the severe odor emergency at the place in dire need of these devices?

3. Is there a hot black market for air fresheners? Why?

4. Do you believe their air freshener really has G.P.S.? (Maybe in this case it stands for "get poacher of scent.")

5. If and when the scent poacher is caught, what will "we" say?

6. Isn't the very invention and use of
    a so-called air freshener ludicrous
    and indicative of one of capitalism's
    fabricated "needs" in light of the fact
    that the greatest air freshener is, of
    course, well, more air.

KEEP ON TRUCKIN' (NOT!)

EVER SEE THIS SIGN on the back of a dump truck?

CONSTRUCTION VEHICLE

DO NOT FOLLOW

Now, honestly, what's a driver supposed
to do?

Slam on the brakes?

Kick it into reverse?

These are perilous options, especially
alongside many fast-moving vehicles on a
superhighway.

Just sayin'.

LOOK BEFORE YOU LEAP

YESTERDAY, after hearing the haunting and apocalyptic "A Day in the Life" by The Beatles on the radio, while approaching the crest of the roadway on the Tappan Zee Bridge (spelled wrong on an official New York State Thruway sign near Port Chester), with radiant Manhattan 10 miles downriver to the left, I saw this sign in the late-afternoon lambent light:

LIFE IS WORTH LIVING

along the right railing, with a "life line" phone number to call.

The signs (I saw one Saturday, coming from the other direction) are an attempt to ward off suicides, or at least potential pedestrian suicidalists (presumably with cellphones, to call the help line). One would think drivers bent on the act would not need to wait until reaching the highest point of the bridge (a lovely bridge, if I may so). Well, come to think of it, why would anyone need to reach the highest point of the bridge before leaping? Certainly, it would not be necessary in terms of the efficacy of the leap. A leap even at the first locus over water seems plenty high enough to do the desperate deed.

I also wondered: why limit signs like this to dramatic venues and vistas such as the Tappan Zee Bridge or the famously suicide-prone Golden Gate Bridge? Are there not landward temptations to self-extinction? Indeed there are. LIFE IS WORTH LIVING signs should be posted just as pointedly at the entranceways to workplaces, government offices, retail stores, churches, homes, rocky cliffs, flat plains, and at the doors of your local Wal-Mart, Target, The Home Depot, or other

SEEING THE SIGNS

big-box store. And who but my eponymous graffiti artist who goes by the tag of LIFE should paint these vivifying signs?

Before you get all fretful about my mental state, let me add these are not lugubrious musings. Far from it.

Life is worth living.

I see the signs everywhere.

(A parenthetical word on bridges. *Pons* is the Latin word for bridge. *Pontifex*, a word for pope, literally in Latin means "one who makes a bridge." So does this mean I have been pontificating? Or am I simply bridging the gap between the quotidian and the nodding head of numinous?)

SEEING THE SIGNS

SIGNAGE

SPOTTED, ON A SIGN, at the outer gateway
to Tipperary Hill:

EXPANDING

HELP WANTED

Presumably, the employer does not discriminate against thin people.

Is one of the job qualifications a propensity on the part of the employee to eat a dozen doughnuts every morning (a propensity that becomes a fulsome reality)?

SIGNS OF
THE NIGHT

TONIGHT'S WALK:

Last summer's swimming pool, alabaster, empty, silent, bathed in light. Not one echo of August's rowdy, tense crowd simmering in a cauldron of raw longing, restlessness, and a dash of suspicion. Black elongated crosses demarcate depths and diving areas at the far end. A black wrought-iron fence guards the perimeter of the pool.

The empty pool strikes a monumental pose. It looks like some kind of shrine with its radiance and stillness. A shrine to what? Snowflakes aimlessly fly about in the brisk wind. What if the pool were a sacred shrine, a local Taj Mahal? What if someone proclaimed The Burnet Park Pool as a tourist venue, designed by, say, Frank Gehry or Frank Lloyd Wright? Just saying so, people would think about it differently. But I don't need such proclamations. It is luminous and miraculous, just as it is.

Walking back home, the "clean, well-lighted place" (Hemingway's phrase) behind me, I see graffiti on a small concrete-block building housing electrical equipment. (Ever

since my trips to Berlin, Germany, I'm more
open-minded about graffiti.) The tag is:

LIFE

in urban blocky font, in black spray paint.

The "i" is not dotted.

Where the dot on the "i" would be, is a
small x.

Which makes me wonder, yet again.

SEEING THE SIGNS

WRONG EXIT

THE SIGNS WERE NOT THERE. Or I did not see them. Well, actually the signs were there. I misread them. I expected more overt, more blatant exit warnings. (Are they "warnings"? More like proclamations, declarations. Not so much Good News, as News. Do with the information what you will.) So I kept going. But it began to feel not quite right. Sure enough, at the rest stop I consulted a map on the wall. I had overshot the exit. I exceeded my expectation. I now had to make the wrong exit the right exit. I took a bridge, of majestic beauty, even as my anxiety rose like the bluish spires holding up the cables. I headed north. I backtracked. I found my way, even though it was not *the* way. I met my party. It was all relative ("all relative," an oxymoron if there ever was one). So I guess wrong was righted.